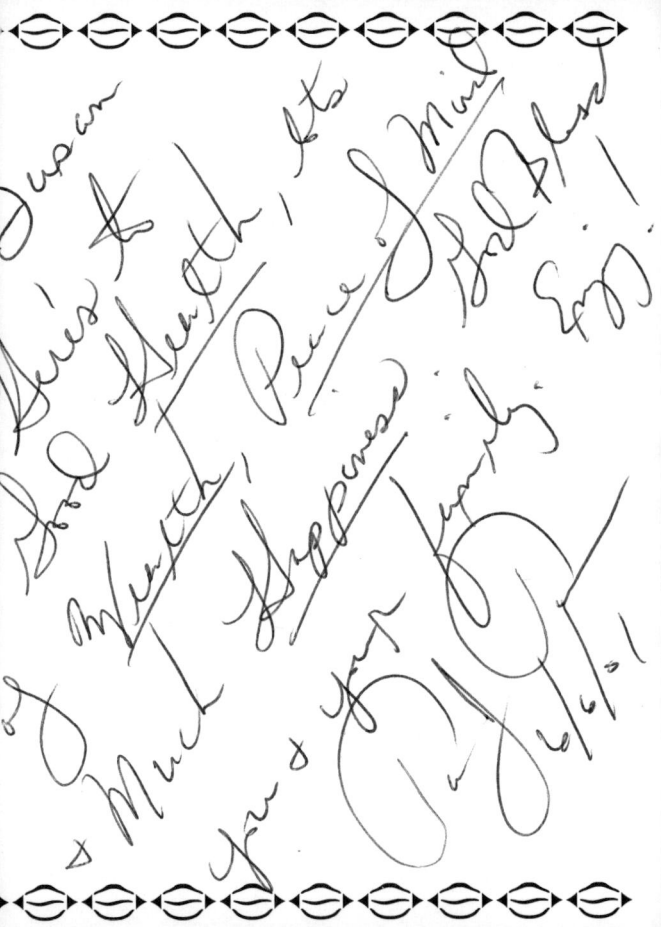

Also by TONI J. TURNER

Love Gone Wrong

A 'FRIEND' BOOK

Friend Publishing Company

Chicago, IL

Tomorrow

My heart does not ache
from my past
I move forward with my life
No time to waste on regrets
Everyday a new
Another day to try harder
to be better, to improve,
to succeed, to fall in love
What a difference a day makes

Love Gone Wrong

*Wisdom From The Soul
Quotes From My Friends*

Wisdom From The Soul
Quotes From My Friends

TONI J. TURNER

Friend Publishing Company

Chicago, IL

Copyright © 1997 by Toni J. Turner

All rights reserved. No part of this book may be reproduced or utilized in whole or part by any means, electronic or mechanical, including photocopying, recording, or by any retrieval system now known or hereafter invented, without written permission from the publisher. Inquires should be addressed to Friend Publishing, c/o Toni J. Turner, 60 East Chestnut 311, Chicago, Illinois, 60611.

Published in the United States of America

Friend Publishing
Wisdom From The Soul
Quotes From My Friends

Cover Design: Lamont Garett
Edited by: Nancy A. Kuehn
Page Composition: Robert Weber

ISBN 09643316-8-3

IN FONDEST MEMORY OF

my beloved aunt, Katherine E. Busch
and
my dearest friend, Jon G. Williams

Special Thanks!

My Right Hand
Nancy A. Kuehn, Editor

Much thanks to 19 at 4 N Da Mornin'

William Asher
You're always there for me.

Robin Hollins-Shannon
Thank you so much.

Maria Gracias
You are God's Gift to Friendship.

Terry Coleman
Thanks for helping me get started.

My Supporters
I Love You for believing in me.

All My Friends
I could not have done it without you!

If I'm stepping on your toes,
Please move your feet!!

This book is dedicated
to living life to the fullest.

My friends say the funniest things.
They don't realize how famous they are.
God's gifts, quick wit and humor have
kept us alive. So, we should be good to
ourselves; we should be happy.

You have to feel it
to understand it.

–T

We don't know how smart we are...
until we listen to ourselves.

–T

There are many things you can give me,
but until you give me your heart,
it will never be the right thing.

–L. Y. Sims

My Momma used to tell me
there are eight men for every woman.
Some Heffa got all my men.

–T. Carter

You could have been my Prince.
You chose to be a frog.

–Toni

You never learned to love.
Now you are afraid to try.

–Tina

Where are all the Good Men?
You have plenty to do until they come.

–Toni

You must be ready when
Right comes along.

–Tina

You have to be a Big Boy
to play with a Big Girl.

–Toni

If I want to play a game
I'll go buy one.

–Toni

Instead of looking at my outer,
look at my inner.

—Toni

A person without vices
is Dangerous.

—19 & Toni

Come to me clean
or stay away dirty.

–Buffy X

A woman who takes care of herself
will take care of you in every way.

–T

I would never want to be a Woman.
I appreciate all the things a Woman goes
through, but it's too much fun being on
the receiving end.

–L. Garrett

I want to be pursued,
courted and wooed.

–Eva

A good date is
a good book and
a long hot bath.

–The Girls

I want someone that makes my
heart pound and my pants dance.

–R.Gustafson

I want a man to have self-respect
and to treat me very special.

–N. Kuehn

A man is not
the most important thing
in a woman's life,
her own security is.

—Toni

Men do what they want to do,
when they want to do it.

– Vermell

No expectations.
No disappointments.

– Tina

I look my best when I'm at my worst.
It's called Pride.

–W. Asher

I'm everything you're too lazy to be.
That's why you don't like me.

–Tina

Everything good begins with you.

                                      –Toni

Strive for perfection
because even if you fail
you will be better than
if you hadn't tried.

                                      –R. Lewis

You have a long way to go
and a short time to make it,
So do it Now!

–D. Mack

Life is conquering one crisis and
moving on to the next and
grabbing happiness in-between.

–Vada

Shoulda,
Coulda,
Woulda,
and Gonna do means,
"What are you waiting for?"

–Toni

It's your drive that keeps you alive.

–J. Jones

People don't fail; they stop trying.

—Toni

If at first you don't succeed,
try something harder.

—Toni

You have to keep going at it
cause it ain't gonna come to you.

–R. Wheeler

No matter how much I'm envied,
I'm going to a level where it doesn't matter.

–19

What helps you when you did
Your best?
Your heart keeps you to the test.

–Toni

Just remember—
your job is a stepping stone
not a tombstone.

–W. Asher

God can't bless you
if you let the devil depress you.

–V. Andrews, A. Jacobs

Your problem is,
"you think you're cute."
No.... your problem is
You think I'm cute.

– G. Taylor

The energy one spends on jealousy
is time one can spend
improving oneself.

– Toni

I thank God for my enemies.
They keep me sharp.

–E. Turner

Don't let their ugly ways
make you ugly!

–Toni

People who have no sunshine
in their lives always want to
rain on your parade.

–J. Houston

Every time you bend over
they want you to fall.

–My Father, A. Turner

If they don't get you in the wash,
they will try to get you in the rinse.

–E. Crooms

No one is going to lick your wounds.
You have to heal yourself.

–Toni

I refuse to let my life be a trash can.

–E. Turner

Every person's butt
you think you have to kiss
is a waste of time.

–Tina

Be First Class in everything you do.
It represents you.

−19

You think I'm short don't you?
When I stand on my wallet I'm real tall.

–A Short Man

A mother can take care of ten children.
Ten children cannot take care of a Mother.

–My Aunt Kate

Teenagers

Take them to the farm and
leave them there until their
minds catch up with their bodies.

–B. Whitfield

A Mother to a Son

You cannot play games with the player.

–L. Smedley

God knew what he was doing
when he made a woman's breast.

–T. James

Who knows a struggle better than a Woman with Peace of Mind.

–Toni

If I could do it all over again-
I'd replace him with a mink.

–W. Asher

If you ain't having any fun,
it's your own damn fault.

> –A Lady at the salon

I was so busy being her friend,
I didn't notice she wasn't mine.

> –E. Turner

Women are their own worst enemies sometimes.

–Toni

I can smell an insecure woman.

–Tina

A person who has a lot of friends is looking for trouble.
A person who has no friends is trouble.

–L.Y. Sims

Don't tell your business and mind your own business.

–P. Lockhart

If you want a married man for a friend, get ready for his Crazy Wife.

–Toni

Love comes between Lust and Divorce.

–W. Asher

You think you have a man.
Your man is community property.

–O. Dickey

If a man is not doing his sexual homework,
he's studying somewhere else.

–C. Chandler

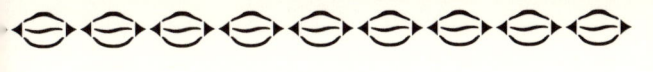

My mother told me not to marry him because I'd have to change his diaper for life.

–J. Corley

One day can ruin a lifetime.

–19

If it were not for
the head in my pants,
the one on my shoulders
would think more clearly.

–J. Jones

No matter how beautiful you are,
all men close their eyes.

—G. Payne

A stiff erection has no conscience.

—G. Payne

The only thing

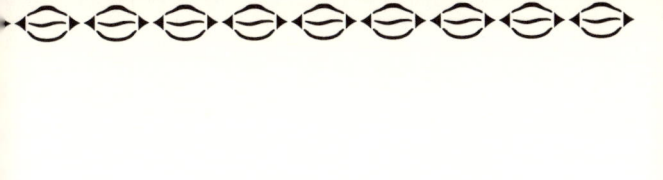

r 2:00 a.m. is legs.

–Vada

He does not want to get married.
He just wants Some.

—19

He thinks he has more balls
than a pool table.

—J. Corley

Never lend a man money.
He loses face. The relationship goes in the toilet and you never get your money back.

–C. Chandler

A man cannot be a Dog unless you let him. If he is a Dog you are the Dog catcher.

–Toni

You are what you sleep with.

–Toni

If she's not good enough to marry,
she's not good enough to sleep with.

–A. Winn

The only thing you don't have to have
is sex.

–19

Sometimes women should just grab *their* balls.

–19

Celibacy = Sexual Fasting

–Buffy X

The only thing a man can do by himself is make mistakes.

–T. Bowman

An insecure man is intimidated by a strong woman.

–B. Beasley

By the time men turn around
to go to the well,
the world will be a living hell.

–T

We could sleep with our doors unlocked
if it were not for men.

–T

You let a rattlesnake in your house;
now you don't know where to step
without your gun.

–O.T. Stephens

You didn't raise me,
so don't raise your hand to me.

–O.T. Stephens

I live my life to the point
where you will always miss me,
but I will never miss you
when it's over.

–Toni

In life you may not get
all that you pay for,
but you will certainly pay
for all that you get.

–M. Long

You keep falling and hitting your head,
maybe one day you'll fall and hit your head
on a smart rock.

–G. Seagent

How many times do you have to be smacked
to realize it hurts?

–L. Chenault

A Cheating Man

If you think my number
is 911 for entertainment,
you dialed the wrong number.
Call your wife!

–Jason & Tina

Is there a sign on my butt that reads,
married men apply here?

–Jason

No Compromise

If you cannot be a good man,
you can be someone else's man,
...but not my man.

–Toni

My head won't bend that low
to kiss your a__.

–P. Smith

The time you waste
on a worthless relationship
that's going nowhere,
you could work an extra job
to get you somewhere.

–Toni

Dust off your Dreams!

–Toni

Depend on God,
yourself and the
almighty dollar.

–K. Jones

Get rid of the wrong in your life.
Make room for the right.

–Toni

You don't have to waste your time getting back at someone, because what goes around comes around, and you will be there to see it.

–Toni

Nothing can be gained by using the good fortune of another person for your own convenience.

–Toni

You'll close the door once more and forget they were ever there.
Some aren't worth remembering.

—Toni

If it ain't right leave it alone.
Get over it and move on.

—Toni

I can respect a person
I don't like.
I cannot like a person
I don't respect.

–M. Gracias

You were down so low,
you could not get up—
the perfect place to begin
to pray.

–Toni

God will send you what you need
when you need it.

–Toni

My first husband may have died in Vietnam. He never got a chance to grow up; I never got a chance to meet him. That's why so many women in their 40's are single. Our young men were sacrificed for old men's greed.

–Tina

You must take the positive
from the negative
and make it work for you.

–Toni

I've met some fools,
but I never stayed around long enough
to become one.

–Toni

If you think I'm a fool,
you are one.

–L.Y. Sims

We can only help those
who want to be helped.

—M. Williams

All the money in the world
cannot hide selfishness,
loneliness and rudeness.

—Tina

Sometimes you have to fall,
so when you get up,
you will walk the right way.

–Toni

Always be kind.
You never know when
you may want to go back.

–Toni

Turn the table to see
yourself through another's eyes.

–Toni

If you are going to fall,
you have to have a cotton ball to fall on
so you won't hurt yourself.

–J. Houston

Never gamble on the new
when the old is good to you.

–T

I've never been lonely by myself,
but I've been lonely with someone.

–B. Skeens

God will pull you through.

–Faith

Nobody knows you until
you are with someone or
you have something.

–M. Smith

Strive for Better.
Better me.
Better life.
Better we.

–Toni

The simple things in life:
Touching, talking, giving, feeling good.

–Toni

A Man to a Woman

I know I can Love You.
Love You Good.
Love You Strong.
Love You Forever!

–My Friend

As long as you know
you are doing right,
Right won't let you down.

              –R. Johnson

We live to die,
so live for No Regrets.

                    –Toni

Remember, only if you let them.

–Toni

You are putting all the
emphasis on the man
instead of yourself.

—Toni

Sometimes
you can't change
what you started out with.

—Vermell

Infidelity is Unforgivable

–T. Coleman

Never let your weakness for the wrong lover kill your passion for a Good Life.

–Love Gone Wrong

Marriage

Did it.
Done it.
Don't want it.

– M. Gracias

Eventually the a__ climbs
up on the shoulders.

– Tina

A Divorce

Hazel ... Your maid
Higgens...Your butler
and Ho.....
don't live here no more.
Betty doesn't either.... the cook.

–Toni

What you took for granted yesterday, you may wish you had today.

–Toni

Love will make you or break you.

–C. Grant

God gave a woman something
he did not give a man—
A sixth sense.
Listen to it and it will never
steer you wrong.

–A Friend

Never settle for less;
less will never make you happy.

–Toni

Some people will have more than you,
some will have less,
but you must be grateful
for what you have.

–E. Jones

No matter what the obstacles, I made it
by being good to myself, by being happy,
and by looking in the mirror and loving me.

–Toni

We are the women
who have rocked and raised America.

–E. Gunter

It's your turn to Laugh a lot and Cry a little.

–Toni

The best revenge is **Success**!

Success is something you create.
Success is handling emotions.
Success is never final.
Success is discipline.
Success is **Sweet**!

–Jason, Toni & 19

Let's just go buy a bottle of Champagne and cross our legs.

–Toni

A Toast!

Here's to Good Health, Lots of Wealth,
Looking Good and the rest will follow.

–Toni

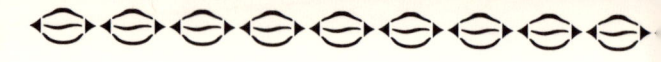

One more thing!

Oil and water ain't never mixed.
Opposites don't attract.

–Toni & 19

My Loves
My Loves who are My Friends
My Friends to the end

We must find a cure for AIDS and Cancer.

–Toni Turner

ABOUT THE AUTHOR

Toni J. Turner, author and publisher of *Love Gone Wrong,* has been given the gift to write her second book. Going through a series of personal tragedies, she has opened her heart to release her pain from dealing with so much death. Her family and friends have become her angels. Through them she has learned to pull the positive from the negative to be all she can be. "People must not forget to turn and reach behind them to help the ones that will follow. There are so many empty rooms at the top and they are there for the taking, but everyone has to help. People must start by sharing their blessings and believing that God is Good, all the time!"

God bless you and
thank you for your Support!

I want to thank the "Good Guys".....

Leonard "Buzzy" Chenault
Lamont Garrett
Jay Jones
Harold Lewis
Vincent Stokes

Last but not least, **Robert Weber**

Rob, you are so special! What would I have done without you? You were there to the end.

To Purchase more copies of
Wisdom From The Soul

Please send $12.95 plus $3.00
tax and shipping per copy to:

FRIEND PUBLISHING
c/o TONI J. TURNER
260 East Chestnut 814 9
Chicago, Illinois 60611

Payable to Toni J. Turner

To Purchase more copies of
Love Gone Wrong

Please send $13.95 plus $3.00
tax and shipping per copy to:

FRIEND PUBLISHING
c/o TONI J. TURNER
260 East Chestnut ~~$10~~ 9
Chicago, Illinois 60611

312-944-7498

Payable to Toni J. Turner

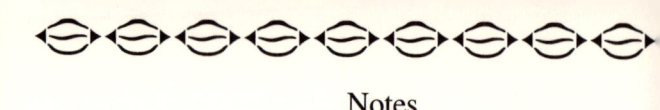

Notes

Notes

Notes